The Murder of Annie Le

Tracy Stromwell

Published by Trellis Publishing, 2021.

While every precaution has been taken in the preparation of this book, the publisher assumes no responsibility for errors or omissions, or for damages resulting from the use of the information contained herein.

THE MURDER OF ANNIE LE

First edition. July 11, 2021.

Copyright © 2021 Tracy Stromwell.

ISBN: 979-8224649884

Written by Tracy Stromwell.

THE MURDER OF ANNIE LE

TRACY STROMWELL

1

Annie Le was a small framed girl attending the prestigious University of Yale for her Doctoral Degree in Pharmacology when she was brutally murdered. Annie was born in San Jose, California to a family of Vietnamese origins. Annie was raised by her aunt and uncle where she was well loved and exceeded all educational standards. Annie attended Union Mine High School and she graduated as the Valedictorian of her class. Fellow classmates voted Annie as being the next "Einstein". Her first major accomplishment was her incredible amount of scholarships. Annie received 160,000$ in scholarship money, that she used to attend the University of Rochester in the state of New York. When she attended the University of Rochester her major was Cell Developmental Biology and her minor was Medical Anthropology. Her studies were aimed at finding treatment for diabetes and different forms of cancer. She was accepted to the graduate program in Yale, which would have left her with a doctorate degree in Pharmacology. This would have allowed her to follow out her dreams of making giant medical milestones in the community.

Annie was hungry for knowledge and she was determined to change the medical community with scientific breakthroughs. Although her passion was primarily medical, she was an academic writer as well. In the February of 2009 she published an article in Yale Medical School's Magazine. The ironic title of this article was "Crime and Safety in New Haven". This article was based on campus safety and it looked at the amount of robberies in New Haven, compared to other cities that housed Ivy Level schools. It advised students on the different campus safety methods such as; the buddy system, utilizing campus police, and avoiding drugs and alcohol. Her article included an interview with Yale's police Chief. In the interview Chief James Perrotti states "pay attention to where you are and avoid portraying yourself as a potential victim." Annie was quoted as stating "In short, New Haven is a city and cities have their perils, but with a little street smarts, one can avoid becoming yet another statistic." Perrotti mentioned that victims of a crime should always make not of their attacker's shoes. "It's important to take not of the attacker's physical appearance, especially the shoes. The shoes are very important because they can shed the clothing along the way... shoes are unique." How does an intelligent and well-versed student like Annie Le get murdered?

Annie Le was the young age of 24 when she was last seen on September 8, 2009. This was only days before her wedding. On the morning of September 8, she left her apartment and took the Yale transit to the Sterling Hall of Medicine. At about 10:00 a.m. Annie Le was seen walking from the Sterling Hall to another building on Campus, on Amistad Street. She left all of her belongs including her cell phone, purse, credit cards, and cash at Sterling Hall. The building on Amistad Street was the campus research laboratory, a place that Annie spent a great deal of time in. She made the walk between buildings hundreds of times and it was not unfamiliar to her. Security cameras were used to determine the time that Annie Le entered the building, and the fact that she never left. On the night of Tuesday, September 8, Annie had not returned back home. It was around 9:00 p.m. when one of Annie Le's five roommates called the police to inform them of her disappearance.

Since her roommates were aware of her plans to use campus transit to get to the school that morning, that is where the Police began their investigation. Security tapes confirmed her entrance into the research lab, and police closed the entire building for investigation. The police took Annie's disappearance extremely seriously, they closed buildings down and searched through the dump where Yale's garbage is burned. Investigators were looking for any clue that gave any indication to Annie's disappearance. The search included the local New Haven Police Department, The Connecticut State Police Department, and the Federal Bureau of Investigation.

On Thursday September 10, the FBI was reviewing images from closed circuit cameras while Annie Le's friends, fiancé, professors, colleagues, and family searched through Yale's campus. Authorities were tearing apart dumpsters, trash bins, and rooms to find any type of evidence that could point to where Annie went. The FBI was not only searching the campus but her apartment building as well. When Yale's spokesmen Tom Conroy was asked for his opinion on whether or not there could have been foul play he responded with the statement "There's no evidence of it at this time." The problem with Conroy's response was the fact that out of Yale's 70 different camera's none of them showed Annie leaving Yale's Laboratory, creating a contradictory statement. The only explanation that would explain why the cameras didn't catch Annie leaving, was when the fire alarm that went off in the building, and many different people were seen leaving. Authorities speculated whether or not she left the building when the fire alarm went off and left in a crowd of people. Her wedding was quickly approaching, and she could have gotten cold feet.

As the search continued over the next few days, the community became very afraid of Annie's welfare. Yale's campus came together and offered a 10,000-dollar reward for anyone who had information leading to Annie's whereabouts. Annie's story quickly went viral, her story was being told around the nation. Her disappearance was one of the top stories on the news, and there were reporters swarming Yale's campus and Annie's apartment. The University's spokeswoman, Sharon Dickman reported Annie Le as being 4 foot 11 inches tall and approximately 90 pounds. Annie was of Asian decent and had brown hair and eyes. Friends of Annie's said it was unlikely that she had gotten cold feet about her upcoming wedding. She was described as marrying her college sweetheart, Jonathan Widawsky. Facility described Annie as being "smart, fun loving, and endlessly energetic." As the search for Annie continued, officers began to re-focus their energy and resources on the laboratory in the building on Amistad Street. On Saturday September 12, 2009 investigators found bloody clothing hidden on the inside of a ceiling tile in the lab. Five days after Annie's disappearance she was found. Found on the day that would have been her wedding day,

September 13, 2009. Her body was found dumped behind a utility panel in the basement of the building on Amistad Street. Police determined it would be difficult for anyone to commit this murder without a laboratory badge, making a much smaller pool of subjects.

Annie's autopsy showed that the cause of her death was asphyxiation. The exact terminology written on the autopsy report was "traumatic asphyxia due to neck compression" In the beginning of the investigation the exact details of the body where withheld from the public. It was later released that Annie's body was found upside down, her bra was pushing upwards towards her head and her underwear was at her ankles. Forensic research determined that before she was strangled, her collarbone and jaw were broken. Police were investigating anyone with a Yale ID, as it was the only way to enter the basement of the laboratory. Police focused on Yale faculty and students when trying to identify the culprit of this murder. Janet Widawsky, her future mother in law stated "Annie was a passionate young scientist who wanted to save the world. A life cut too short." On Tuesday night the police held a news conference where they announced that the person of interest in Annie Le's murder case, they named Raymond Clark III as their primary suspect. Clark's name went viral, and immediately became public due to the media coverage of the press conference. On Wednesday, September 16, The Register began interviewing friends and family of Raymond Clark. One of his fellow high school students went on record to say "He was the nicest kid – very quiet, but everyone liked him. I can't believe he could do this. I am sick to my stomach." Clark was a 24-year-old laboratory Technician at Yale. According to Laura Smith, the President of Local 34 (the union that represents the technical workers) "One colleague murdered, and another accused -it's the talk of the medical school. Nobody could talk about anything else." It was the University's Deputy of Security that made sense of Annie's connection to Clark. The basement required a special electronic ID cards and codes, the part of the basement where Annie was found took an extra level of clearance to get too. When they reviewed the cards swiped the day that Annie was murdered, Annie swiped her card and Clark swiped his right after.

When Police arrested Raymond Clark III, they did not state a motive or any type of case against him. According to Police Chief James Lewis "It was not a domestic crime. It was a workplace crime" Clark was held at a three-million-dollar bond and his lawyer stated that Clark would be pleading not guilty to the murder of Annie Le. The death of a Yale student and accusation of a Yale Technician made a large impact on the community and questioned Yale's safety measures on campus. Yale's President put out a written statement that read, "This incident could have happened in any city, in any university, or in any workplace. It says more about the dark side of the human soul than it does about the extent of security measures. Even though this was not a consequence of a security lapse, there is no question that it touched off sensitivities of a community and brought to the surface anxiety about security in various parts of the campus, in particular the medical school." Yale did take further security measures after Annie's body was discovered and it was hard to determine if anything would have actually prevented Annie Le's murder. It is unknown if tighter security would have changed the outcome in this case, but Yale now does complete background checks on all new employees.

As Clark's name gained momentum in the media more and more people came to speak against him. One of his high school girlfriends was interviewed with the television show Good Morning America. She told hosts of GMA that Clark would become angry often and he would frighten her, it was not unusual for him to become physical with her. When she broke up with Clark she had to be escorted to her car from the school. This woman filed a police report on Clark where she stated that he had forced her to have sex with him, but she did not press charges, she just came out to tell her story. The details behind Clark's arrest were not given to the public immediately, but eventually it was reported that there were several articles of clothing that linked him to Annie Le. In the

Police's arrest case against Raymond Clark they stated that investigators found a t-shirt with blood that was strikingly similar to the blue T-shirt that Clark was wearing the same day that Annie went missing. When police were conducting their investigation, they found a box of hygiene wipes on a cart outside of the laboratory. The clothing in the ceiling tiles consisted of; a lab coat with blood stains and DNA from Annie Le and an unknown male, Annie's athletic sock, a blood-stained rubber glove that had Annie's DNA on it, a pair of work boots that were labeled as "Ray-C" and a blue shirt that matched Clark's shirt. Some of this evidence had both blood and hair stuck to the fibers of the clothing. The police used this evidence to obtain a search and seizure warrant for Raymond Clark. The police swabbed the inside of his mouth, took body hair, fingernail clippings, and fingerprints during this search. It was not long until police confirmed that the unknown DNA in the basement and on the clothes matched Raymond Clark III's. The hygiene wipes were most likely used for cleaning up any bloodstains on the floor. Chemicals revealed that there were in fact bloodstains on different floors of the laboratory, including the floor that Annie was killed on.

When Clark was interviewed by the Police for the first time he was noted as having a scratch on his face and left bicep. Clark claimed that he was scratched by a cat and it had left marks throughout his body. Not only was his DNA all over the clothing, he dropped a green pen underneath Annie Le's body. The blood on the pen was matched to Clark, and the ink was matched to ink on a timesheet that Clark used to sign in on earlier that day. There was a lot of controversy over releasing the court records and police documents. It went before a judge where a judge determined that this information could be released to the public as it would not interfere with the trial. The Police were putting together and extremely strong case against Raymond Clark and went as far as reconstructing Clarks activities on the day that Annie Le went missing and was killed. Clark did not help himself after Annie's body was found. Rachel Roth, Annie's fellow alerted the Yale Police Officer,

Sabrina Wood about the hygiene wipes. These wipes were what drew the FBI back to the room. Clark was noted as leaving the room several times, and he went to the cart and moved the wipes from one side to the other, covering up the bloodstains by turning them towards the wall. Clark tried to keep his cool by talking to police officers and volunteering information. Clark told officer Jennifer Garcia that he was there when Annie entered the laboratory at 10:30 am and watched her leave at approximately 12:30 p.m. even though the cameras did not show Annie leaving the building. Investigators knew that Clark was the person in charge of taking care of the animals in the laboratory where Annie was hidden. Clark told FBI agents "We never saw each other out of work". Although authorities were well aware of the DNA connections between Clark and Le. they did not make a big deal of the connections while gathering evidence and creating their case. They continued to ask the public for information pertaining to Annie Le's disappearance.

As the investigation was continuing family and friends were busy setting up and attending memorial services in remembrance and love of Annie Le. There was an hour-long service held at near her Fiancé's synagogue where 300 people attended. This happened to be the same place that Annie and her fiancé, Jonathon, were to be married. Many of Annie's friends and family stood up to speak in her honor, remembering her for the loving, bubbly, and energetic girl she was. Annie and her fiancé had plans to honey moon in Greece, and rather than taking the trip to Greece he was planning her funeral. Annie's future mother in law stated "I recall her cherishing the plans for her upcoming wedding, as well as her life with Jonathan, also 24. Le was animal love and she had ones rescued a group of abandoned kittens on Long Island." Her mentor described Annie as sweet and always smiling. "Everyone got along with her, she's always smiling and laughing." Annie was smart, and she was remembered by many as having a goal to regenerate tissue for people with degenerative bone disease. Annie had aspirations to work as an investigator or as a professor, teaching what she loved. Annie's funeral was held in a private Mass in the foothills of the Sierra Nevada's near her hometown. Her mother read a poem that she had written to her daughter in Vietnamese after hearing the news of her murder and the priest attempted to reconcile her vibrant life with her violent death. Her brother Chris acted as a translator at different parts of the Mass. There were more then 600 people who attended Annie's service, proving just how much her community loved her and appreciated her. Unfortunately, her services were also flooded with the media, as her death caused eruption through the nation. Eight pallbearers wearing white to her casket to a hearse where she was buried nearby in Rescue.

Clark was held at MacDougall-Walker Correctional Institution in Suffield, Connecticut as he awaited trail. He stood in front of the Superior Court on October 6, 2009 but he did not enter any plea when given the charges. It was not until January 26, 2010 that Raymond Clark III plead not guilty in front of the court. It took numerous months for his hearing to proceed, due to the fact that not all of the lawyers had the materials pertaining to the case. He was scheduled to attend a pre-trial on March 3, 2010 in New Haven, Connecticut. A pre-trial evidentiary hearing was scheduled for July 26, 2010. Clark's trial continued into the year 2011 when he finally made a guilty plea. In March of 2011, Clark plead guilty to Annie Le's murder and took a sentence of 44 years in prison. He also entered an Alford Plea to the charges of sexual assault on Annie Le. On March 17, 2011 friends and family traveled to hear Raymond Clarks sentencing for murder. Superior Court Judge Roland Fasano went on record as saying, "The suffering and the anguish of the families is heartbreaking. For murder, 44 years to serve. For attempted sexual assault in the first degree, 20 years to run concurrently." This sentence would keep Clark incarcerated into the year 2053 and according to the Supervisory Assistant to the State Attorney, John Waddock, "Who will be there waiting for him? Most, if not all of his family will be gone. He will have no real future."

There was quite a crowd at Clarks Sentence Hearing. Both Clarks mother and father sat behind him in the crowd and his mother was seen wiping tears from her eyes as the judge announced his sentence. Clarks father was the only family member on Raymond Clarks side to offer a statement, "My family's deepest sympathies to the Le family. The grief and tears we shed are equal for your family as well as ours. The events of September 2009 devastated two families and shocked a nation. No parent can imagine or prepare for losing their daughter to violence or having their son commit such a horrible crime. Ray was raised in a loving and supportive household and was a good son. I say this to underscore how shocked we were to hear that Ray committed this horrible, senseless offense...This is not the Ray we have known and raised; we can't explain or make sense of this. I will never understand, as I know that Ray does not understand, how this could have happened.

On the opposite side of Clark there were around 20 members from Annie Le's family. Both of Annie's parents delivered statements right before the sentence was imposed upon Clark, which actually cause tears to build up in Clark's eyes. Annie's mother Vivian Van Le said, "Annie was a beautiful, brilliant young woman and the world will never know what she had to offer. I will never see her walking down the aisle. I will never hug Annie again...I only see my Annie in my dreams". Annie's father, Hoang Le did not have much to say but he is on record as saying, "I hope as a result of my daughter's death there will be greater security provided for all students on campus as well as safe working environments." It may have been one of Annie's Uncles and Cousins that gave the most heart wrenching statement. In front of the court Annie's Uncle, Robert Nguyen, the man who raised Annie Le read a statement from him and his wife, "I wish to ask this court to sentence Raymond Clark to forfeit every day of his natural life, as Annie did at his hands, and nothing less in prison." Annie's cousin Ryan Nguyen followed his parents' statement with saying "The family looked forward to sharing and celebrating the happiest moment of Le's life at the wedding. Instead, on the flight home from New Haven, I remember how painful it was for me to know that (Le's) coffin would be flying home on that very same day."

The most powerful statement given that day was given from Raymond Clark himself, even though it did not give the Le family any peace. He did not disclose any motive for killing Annie or give the family any answers as to why he felt the need to strangle their daughter. In front of both families and the judge he stated, "I take full responsibility for my actions. I alone am responsible for the death of Annie Le and causing tremendous pain to all who love and cared about Annie. I am truly sorry I took Annie away from her friends, her family, and most of all her fiancé. I have always tried to do the right thing and stay out of trouble, but I failed. I took a life and continued to lie about it while Annie's friends, family and fiancé sat and watched. I really never wanted to harm anyone or cause emotional pain to anyone. All I wanted was to be a good son, a good brother and a good fiancé, but again, I failed. I blame only myself and there are no excuses for what I have done. Annie was and will always be a wonderful person, by far a better person than I will ever be in my life. I'm sorry I lied, I'm sorry I ruined lives, and I am sorry for taking Annie Le's life." This statement was unsatisfying, and it did not give any answer as to what caused him to do what he did to Annie. Many members of the Le family felt that Clarks sentence was not harsh enough or satisfactory enough. The family was reminded that Clark did not have any opportunity to get out of jail on parole and he would remain incarcerated for most of his natural life. There were some members of the Le family that thought Clarke deserved the death penalty or at least life in prison. Annie Le's brother stated there is no punishment capable of making him feel better, but he does hope that Raymond Clark will eventually realize the extent of his actions.

Annie's family's lawyer, Joe Tacopina stated "The investigation has provided us with an incentive to continue moving forward in the civil arena to insure Annie's death is not in vain." After the trial was over the University praised everyone who worked on Annie's case and said that they will continue to honor Annie's name through a fellowship that was established in her name. The Le family filled a civil lawsuit against the University of Yale on the grounds that Yale did not provide women with adequate protection and security in the lab building. They believed that additional security at the lab would have stopped Annie's slaying. The Le family hired another lawyer, Paul Slager who took on this case. The family also stated that Yale officials should have known that Clark was potentially dangerous as he had shown aggressive behavior towards another woman. He was known as a controlling man, he viewed the lab and the mice as his own territory. Yale's lawyers defended the incident, claiming that they had no previous knowledge or information that indicated Clark was capable of murder. Annie's relatives have gone on record in court to say "What should have been a joyous wedding suddenly turned into mourning the loss of a woman whose research included finding new treatments for chronic diseases. She was a doctoral pharmacology student who worked on a team that experimented on mice as part of research into enzymes that could have implications for the treatment of cancer, diabetes and muscular dystrophy." The family officially won their settlement against Yale University and Yale agreed to pay 3 million dollars for the wrongful death of Annie Le.

SHE MADE THEM KILLERS: THE TRUE STORY OF BARBARA OPEL

13

JESSI NIXON

In 2001, Barbara Opel murdered a 64 year old man – but committed the act by paying a group of five teenagers, including her own 13 year old daughter, to do her dirty work. On April 13, Jerry Duane Heiman was ambushed by the small group, who attacked him with knives and baseball bats to complete the job. Opel's younger children, 7 and 11 years old, followed their mother's instructions to assist the teenagers by mopping up Heiman's blood.

The body was discovered eight days later, in a shallow grave located just ten miles away from the house.

Blind trust

Heiman, who had been diagnosed with terminal cancer, had hired Opel in the fall of 2000 to care for his 89 year old mother, who was afflicted with advanced Alzheimer's disease. A Boeing retiree, Heiman provided Opel and her children with something they'd never experienced before – stability.

The brash, overweight mother and her three young children – Heather, 13, an 11 year old son and a 7 year old daughter – had resided in 22 places in just seven years, including a stint where they lived out of the family car. Welfare authorities reported that Opel had been evicted from 10 different apartment buildings for non-payment of rent.

Heiman should have been a godsend. Opel and her children moved into the basement of his home in Everett, Washington, while he lived upstairs with his mother. However, Opel was more than just ungrateful – she was abrasive. Although she frequently initiated arguments with Heiman, he allowed himself to trust her. She was even permitted to write cheques from his bank account to cover household expenses.

But his faith gave Opel some insight into Heiman's prosperity – and she wanted the $40,000 in his bank account for herself. He'd made the money through the sale of a house, and according to prosecutors, the large sum was enough to give her a motive for Heiman's murder.

Hatching a plan

Described by her own sister as "brain-dead," Opel came up with a murderous plot to eliminate Heiman and take control of his finances – but her plan depended on the help of her bright young daughter, Heather, and her group of friends.

Although she'd been raised into a nomadic kind of lifestyle, Heather was a smart, motivated young woman. Her grades were high, and she excelled as a basketball player. In fact, her biggest dream was to someday star in the WNBA – but in the short term, she was hoping to get a dirt bike.

Just a month before Heiman was killed, an entry in Heather's diary showed how she planned to get the bike of her dreams – "so my mom said if I helped kill Jerry I can go get one."

Heather's friends would also receive rewards for their roles in Opel's scheme – she promised cash payments to anyone Heather could recruit to help carry out the murder. Heather managed to find a female friend, Marriam Diane Oliver, who was also 14. Along with three other adolescent boys, the two girls broke into Heiman's room one night in March 2001 armed with bats and knives, but were too scared at the time to carry out Opel's plan.

But just a month later, Heather had managed to pull together a second hit squad to take out her mother's boss. She'd developed a crush on an older boy named Jeff Grote, who was 17 years old, muscular, and worked at the local skating rink.

Opel recognized this crush as an opportunity to bring the strong young man under her wing, and immediately invited Grote to move into the Heiman house with the family – even promising him a private room where he could have sex with her young daughter. He agreed, and found himself under Opel's influence.

She persuaded Grote to put together a new hit team, including his friend Kyle Boston, 15, and Boston's 13 year old cousin – along with Heather and her friend Marriam. In exchange for his participation in the murder, Opel promised, Grote would receive a car and new clothes. The

Bostons would receive $300 to split between them, and Oliver would be given enough money to purchase new skates. Heather, of course, would finally get her dirt bike.

Unusually close

The relationship between Heather and her mother was not your typical mother-daughter bond. According to Heather, the two were unusually close – more like sisters, or friends, than a mother and daughter.

"I just felt like I could tell her anything," she said. "And she was always there with me whenever I went anywhere."

According to Heather's 79 year old grandmother, who relocated to a motel in Everett to regularly visit her daughter and granddaughter in prison, described Heather's childhood as happy – painting a sweet picture of a caring mother who loved to bake chocolate chip cookies with her eager children, laughing together while making a mess of the kitchen.

However, the defense brought in a clinical psychologist who described Heather as "abnormally" loyal and obedient – the kind of child who would likely be unable to stand up to a dominating, controlling mother. This characterization was reinforced by witnesses, including Heather's baseball and basketball coaches. They described how Opel would scream at Heather from the sidelines during games – often bringing the star athlete and "nice kid" to tears.

"I couldn't believe it," said Lane Erickson, who coached a Boys and Girls Club ball team in Everett. "Heather was the only girl on the boys team, and she was the best player by far. The only problem was that the mom would yell and scream at her, and Heather would start crying."

Another coach testified that Opel's out of control, overbearing attitude was so severe that he assigned her the role of assistant coach in an effort to curb her behaviour from the dugout.

Even Heather's father Bill Opel, who divorced Barbara back in 1990, remembered his daughter as being quiet and withdrawn – and maintained that her only downfall was her unfailing allegiance to her domineering mother.

"There's not a right and a wrong way – the only way Heather knows is mom's way," Bill said. "And Heather does not question mom."

Still, allegations of abuse have followed Opel since Heather was born in September, 1987. Not even a year later, neighbours at the Opels' Mill Creek apartment complex were complaining to authorities that she was screaming at her newborn baby.

"The level of violent screaming is escalating," said one anonymous caller. "Recently, one of the neighbours has heard slaps to the baby."

A visit to the apartment was conducted by Child Protective Services (CPS), but reports indicated that the workers found the baby clean and displaying no evidence of abuse. Still, the calls continued – two years later, CPS received a call from the landlord, who said Opel "has been yelling at Heather since the child was three months old."

The landlord added that worried neighbours had also contacted the police, who reported back that the apartment was clean and the toddler was unbruised and well-fed. But the neighbours kept complaining, even advising CPS that Heather and her siblings were being left unsupervised.

According to a former neighbour, Megan Slaker, the kids were often locked out of the house. She would invite them to help her with yard work, and said she prayed for them regularly.

"She just didn't want them in the house, I guess," she said. "You feel compassion for children who you don't think are getting the love and attention they need. I wanted them to feel some love."

Chris Perry lived across the street from Opel and her children for a couple of years. She said Opel had previously lived next door to her best friend, and she wasn't pleased to see the family relocate to her neighbourhood.

"She was a lady I would never forget in my entire life," Perry said. "She was just so mean – screaming at her kids all the time, all hours of the night. You would never hear her lovingly talking to her children."

Opel and Heather's father Bill each accused each other of mistreatment and abuse, and the couple's divorce was described as "an active battleground" by a psychologist. Opel's second marriage has also been compared to a battleground – and even Heather admitted she had a tough time growing up.

"I have some real scars," she said, noting that she began experimenting with drugs like marijuana and ecstasy when she was only 11 years old. "But I felt like I was really starting to pull through it."

She began drinking then, as well, and particularly enjoyed Bacardi spiced rum.

"I shouldn't have done the drugs, and I shouldn't have hung out with the people I did hang out with," she said.

Although Heather claims her mother was not to blame for her misbehaviour, Opel was not a positive influence on her daughter. In February 2001, she hosted a Valentine's Day party for her kids at Heiman's home – and according to one 12 year old guest, the kids were welcome to drink beer, smoke marijuana, use the hot tub in the backyard, and have sex in Opel's bedroom.

While she said she didn't engage in any of this behaviour, her father was furious to learn about the illicit activities – he'd been assured by Opel that night that the party would be safe.

"I'm absolutely shocked – I'm ashamed I let my daughter spend the night there," he said. "I trusted (Opel)."

By that point, Heather was really starting to clean her life up. Her focus had shifted from drugs and alcohol to basketball and other athletics, and she had started working to get her schoolwork on track. She was determined to achieve her dream of playing in the WNBA.

"I sat down and just started writing all my goals," she explained. "I wrote about 100 of them."

During their messy divorce, Bill engaged Opel in a drawn-out custody battle in an attempt to secure at least the right to visit his children. She refused to stick to the agreed-upon visitation and kept the children from him for years, he said. Court records show that in 1997, prosecutors managed to charge her with custodial interference, but the charge was dropped because they felt a jury wouldn't convict.

Eventually, Bill admitted he just gave up, moving to Wenatchee with his new wife and their children.

"I couldn't chase it anymore," he said. "I've just been writing my child-support checks and hoping they go to a good cause. Guess they didn't."

Carrying out the job

On April 13, Jerry Heiman came home to an ambush. The five teenagers attacked him as soon as he stepped in the door, with one cracking him hard on the head with an aluminum bat. He had no idea who the children were, and he started begging for mercy.

"Who are you?" he cried out. "What do you want?"

While the larger teenager beat him with the big bat, two others hit him repeatedly with souvenir bats from the Seattle Mariners. Finally, the two girls appeared with a 10-inch kitchen knife, which they used in turns to stab him until he was dead.

"He looked me straight in my eyes and begged me to help him," Oliver later explained. "All I could do was drop the knife and run and not get him help either."

Oliver had gotten squeamish, and retreated into the basement where Opel was hiding with her two younger kids. But Opel wouldn't let her quit.

"Get up there and do what you're supposed to do," she hollered at the girl until she complied. "You're supposed to be Heather's friend. You're supposed to be there for her!"

When the job was done, Opel and her murderous team celebrated with a nice dinner and a night at the Rodeway Inn – paid for with Heiman's credit card. The very next day, Opel used his checkbook again to rent a truck, packing it up with the dead man's valuables. She didn't get far, though.

Heiman's son Greg had traveled from Arkansas to visit his father in the days after Heiman was murdered. After spending three and a half hours wandering around Sea-Tac Airport waiting for his dad to pick him up, Greg eventually took a shuttle to his father's home in Everett. The scene he discovered was horrifying.

The lights were all off, and the doors were locked. The shades were drawn, so Greg couldn't even see inside the seemingly deserted home. Once he climbed in through a side window, he found his grandmother alone in the house – sitting in her wheelchair, her mouth full of shredded pages from a magazine. All of the furniture was gone, save for a couple of lawn chairs, but the hot tub outside was still running. Later, Greg found dried blood spotted on the garbage can and on the chandelier.

He went looking for his father the next day. Within the week, Heiman's body had been found wrapped in sheets and buried in a shallow grave on the Tulalip Indian reservation. In an attempt to prevent authorities from identifying the body, acid had been poured all over it.

It wasn't long before Barbara Opel was brought in for questioning. She and the five teenagers were quickly charged with the murder.

"That was fun!"

According to the district attorney who prosecuted the case, the teenaged killers were "monsters" who displayed "cold indifference" to what they'd done. Prosecutors attested that after stabbing Heiman, Heather Opel exclaimed in delight, "That was fun! I want to do it again!"

But according to an article from the Seattle Post in August 2002, she learned fast that her actions had very serious consequences.

"In my room, I just sit and stare at my bricks. I'm like, 'look what you got yourself into,'" Heather told reporter M.L. Lyke.

At her sentencing, Heather publicly apologized to the Heiman family – and read aloud a poem she wrote in her cell, lamenting the fact that despite all her efforts to be a "good girl," people still seem to think she's "bad."

"People just look at me that way, and I'm just like, why can't they look at the good side of me?" she said.

Defense attorneys argued that, coming from broken families, the young people were vulnerable and easily swayed by the bullying and abusive tactics demonstrated by Barbara Opel. Still, the judge's determination was that the "hands-on nature" of an attack carried out with clubs and knives made the children candidates for adult court – except for Mike Boston, who was just 13 years old.

Heather, who was 13 at the time of the killing, pleaded guilty and received a sentence of 22 years with no possibility of parole.

"Her mother used her as payment for murder, then commanded her to kill, too" said Seattle attorney Michele Shaw, who argued that Heather had been manipulated fost of her life. "She is a victim herself."

Just 14 years old when she was convicted, Heather will be released from prison at the age of 35. She still hopes to play professional basketball upon her release. She also retains the right to appeal the judge's decision to try her as an adult – and if she wins the appeal, she could cut more than ten years off this 22 year prison term.

"She was responsive, compliant, respectful in every way," said her former principal, Jim McNally. "She was always surrounded by friends. This was a devastating blow to us. To see someone with so much potential in such crisis – it's beyond words."

Marriam Oliver, 14, received 22 years, and 14 year old Kyle Boston was sentenced to 18 years. Boston's cousin Mike will be held in a juvenile prison until he is 21 years old. Heather's boyfriend, Jeffrey Grote, also pleaded guilty and received a sentence of 50 years. In a description he wrote to an online pen pal, Grote claims he is an "easygoing, humorous person," and "a big teddy bear."

At her own trial in 2003, Barbara Opel testified that it was the kids who wanted to kill Heiman – she'd only wanted him to be hurt, she stated. Defense attorneys portrayed Heiman as an abusive drunk.

"I guess I thought that if Jerry got beat up bad he deserved it," she said. "The only thing that had been on my mind was everything the kids and I had been through."

Heiman had mistreated her daughter, Opel claimed, and she'd gotten so fed up with his behaviour that she frequently made comments like, "I wish he was dead" to her family and friends. According to Opel's defense attorney Peter Mazzone, she'd simply gotten swept up in an attack that got out of control.

In his argument, Mazzone said Grote was to blame. He wanted to move in with the Opel's, Mazzone told the jury, but Opel said that if he was to do so, he would need a car to help her run errands like taking the younger children to school. She admitted that after Heiman was killed, she used his credit cards to take the teenagers on a shopping spree.

"I had no way to pay for my kids," she testified when Mazzone asked what she was doing with the dead man's credit cards. "No way else to get food."

She claimed she'd been "horrified" by the murder, stating that if she'd known Grote and his friends had intended to kill Heiman, she would have never let him move into the house. However, once the killing had been carried out, she felt it was her responsibility to protect her daughter, who had been involved.

But according to deputy prosecuting attorney Chris Dickinson, this wasn't the first time Opel had tried to have Heiman killed. He told the jury that Opel had attempted at least four previous plots to murder her employer – and finally managed to convince a group of teenagers who grew up in broken homes to carry out her evil scheme.

"She took them in," he explained, "partied with them, gave them a place to hang out."

Convicted and sentenced

As the jury was unable to reach a unanimous decision after seven hours of deliberation, Opel managed to avoid being sentenced to death – keeping her from going down in history as the first woman on

Washington's death row. While seven jurors supported the prosecution's case for the death penalty, five others felt life in prison was a more appropriate sentence.

According to juror Sally Toffic, one of the five women who served in the trial, the jury spent hours listening to Opel's confession to police and carefully examined all of the evidence – but there was no convincing those who pushed for a life sentence.

"We wanted to make sure we didn't leave a single stone unturned," she said. "But we just got to a point where there was no reason to continue on."

However, Opel still received a life sentence without the possibility of parole, on the conviction of aggravated first-degree murder. Another 12 months was added for her abandoning Heiman's invalid mother, and five additional months for theft. Opel did admit to the jury that she "hated" abandoning the elderly woman, who ended up passing several days without food or water.

"I didn't want to leave her," said Opel, who had helped feed and care for Heiman's mother. "I wanted her to come along with us."

Opel was also banned from having any contact with her children – but her sentence means that she may eventually serve out her sentence in the same prison as her daughter Heather. Once Heather and Oliver turn 18, they would be relocated to Washington Women's Correctional Center in Purdy – the facility where Opel will spend the rest of her life.

"Your fundamental right of seeing your children is lost when you do to your children what Barbara did to hers," said Superior Court Judge Gerald Knight.

Opel wept as the jury's decision was read, whimpering and wrapping her arms around her defense attorney. According to Mazzone, he and partner Brian Phillips had worried throughout the trial, second-guessing all their witnesses and words as if "someone's life depended on it."

"It's the right result," Mazzone said after the verdict was handed down. "Today is Good Friday, and the theme is life."

In order to return a death sentence, the jury would have needed to reach the unanimous conclusion that there were no mitigating circumstances to spare her life – and defense attorney Brian Phillips presented the court with at least five.

Testimony provided by a neuropsychologist and a neuropsychiatrist suggested Opel suffered from impaired brain function – but Toffic admitted that while some jurors believed the argument, others dismissed it as "psychobabble." In her opinion, none of the potential mitigating circumstances was convincing.

"Everyone had their own reason for voting the way they did," she said. "There were a surprising number of different reasons that people had for their vote."

Alternate juror Christine Wintch admitted after the trial that her vote would have been for the death penalty. Although she heard all the testimony presented in the case, she was not part of the jury's deliberations – and Wintch came to her conclusion after learning Opel could potentially serve the majority of her sentence in the same facility as Heather. In fact, a corrections officer reported that during the trial, Opel commented that she hoped to be reunited with Heather in prison so they could continue to "kick ass" there.

However, Superior Court Judge Gerald Knight's recommendation was that Opel not be housed in the same prison as either Heather or her best friend, Marriam Oliver. Since their sentences were handed down, the mother and daughter team have never been in the same facility.

"I hope you rot in hell," said Colleen Muller, Heiman's daughter, looking Opel right in the eyes after the verdict was read. Her brother, Greg Heiman, called Opel "a monster" and "an evil piece of trash."

The siblings also defended their father against the claim that he was an alcoholic, stating that while Heiman had his quirks and "liked his beer, hot cars, and women," he was never abusive.

"He liked to go out to the bars... but for all of that, he was a good man," Muller said.

Maintaining distance

Opel said she still can't describe what went on the night Heiman was killed.

"It's hard to explain how I felt, but I know it was a feeling I never felt before," she said. "It was like I was in some different world."

Heather, on the other hand, has spent a lot of her time in prison reliving the past – thinking back to the night of April 13, 2001. She works out, plays basketball, visits with her grandmother, and reads John Grisham novels, but she can't escape what she did to Jerry Heiman.

"I'd give up my life right now for Jerry to come back, I seriously would," she said. "I always wanted to be famous and be in the newspaper and on TV and stuff, but not like this. I guess my wish did come true – but it had a bad ending to it."

However, she has been able to reconnect with her father while in prison.

"It was a part of my heart that was missing," said Heather. "Everybody in here was like, 'oh yeah, my dad is coming to see me,' and I was thinking, 'yeah, you're so lucky to have a dad.'"

Opel attempted to reach out to her daughter as well, with a written plea from her prison cell in 2013, to be allowed to exchange letters with Heather. Her request was denied, however, by Superior Court Judge Thomas Wynne, who said he was "familiar with the case."

According to deputy prosecutor Chris Dickenson, the ruling was appropriate.

"The last time these two had regular contact," he said, "a man got murdered."

While Heather said her love for her mother remains, their relationship is considerably more complicated after Opel persuaded her to commit a murder.

"In front of the love, there is a whole bunch of hate," she said. "I know that's a strong word, but there's a whole bunch of that."

PORN STAR & KILLER : THE TRUE STORY OF AMANDA LOGUE

ALISON YALE

"I own a lingerie and tanning store. I also host lingerie shows. I will do almost any photo shoot but no porno films. I am fun and energetic. I am looking for paid work." - Amanda' Logue's on-line modeling profile

Amanda Logue had a double life. She was married with a young daughter. But only her husband knew what she was doing on the side to earn money.

Prostitution. Pornography.

She headlined several adult films under the stage name of "Sunny Dae". Together with her bisexual partner, Jason Andrews, the two would reach heights of sexual perversion that would lead them down the path to the ultimate taboo.

Murder.

They would rob and kill tattoo shop owner Dennis "Scooter" Abrahamsen in a shocking crime that made national headlines.

But their motivation wasn't money.

They committed the crime because it made them "hot."

EARLY LIFE

Amanda Dailey was born in the small town of Leesburg, Georgia. Her life goals were simple. She wanted "the two and a half kids, the big house and the wrap around porch. Just have the perfect life."

But things went south for Amanda in her teen years. She got pregnant during her senior year and dropped out of school to have a baby girl. Then her mother would die suddenly the following year.

She would get involved in drugs when her mom died. She would also claim that her daughter's father was abusive.

Things were a mess with numerous domestic interventions by the police.

But that is when she met police officer Lamon Logue. Logue was thirty-years old and eight years the senior of Amanda. The two hit it off as he appeared to be her knight in shining armor.

They began dating and Amanda took a shot at living the normal life. They would go to nice restaurants and to the movies. She found a job at a local car dealership as a secretary. Together, they could work together and create the American Dream.

"Lamon was clearly a good man," forensic psychologist Paula Orange said. "But he was one of those men who fall prey to the charms of a beautiful woman who is down on her luck. They feel the need to fix the woman, the need to be that knight in shining armor but in the end that narrative never works."

Amanda had an itch for more than a domesticated life with a husband and kids. Sure, she wanted a family but something was missing. Some indefinable sense of fun and fulfillment that she wasn't getting at home. Finally, her husband asked her what her lifetime dream was.

Always considered attractive, the bleach-blonde Amanda did not hesitate in answering. She always wanted to be a model.

Lamon encouraged Amanda to pursue her dreams. She answered a few ads and eventually was featured in a small advertising flyer. It was easy, quick money and Amanda enjoyed the work. Gaining more experience, she would get gig after gig and soon the money she was earning through modeling exceeded her salary at the car dealership.

ANOTHER WRONG TURN

Lamon remained the primary breadwinner despite Amanda's blossoming career and their finances took a hit when he was seriously injured in a car accident. The injuries were so severe that he had to go on disability.

Over the following months, the couple needed money. Desperately.

Amanda decided to pursue modeling assignments that were on the seedy side. She claims she simply got "swept up" by the lifestyle as she would be hired for nude photo shoots. This escalated into foot fetish jobs followed by bondage spreads.

Going down a slippery slope, she started having sex with other men on camera. Amanda was now a porn star. The money was easy and quick.

"For one shoot it would only take an hour," Amanda said. "And you could get paid thousands of dollars."

"Like most young women," Orange said. "Amanda saw performing in pornographic videos as an easy way to make cash. But Amanda was a bit older. A twenty-eight year old woman knows exactly what she's doing. It wasn't like she was some naïve eighteen-year-old from Kansas. Amanda had these desires knocking around in her head for a long time. In looking at the clips of her movies, you can see she knows exactly what she's doing. She's enjoying it. She did all of these things because she enjoyed it, whether it was drugs or having sex on camera for money."

By the end of 2007, she was appearing regularly under the name of "Sunny Dae".

Kristen Cameron, a Florida-based model who once worked with Amanda, described her as a "decent person".

"She was professional, prompt, and seemed all around normal," Cameron recalled. "She was nice to me and was a great model! I felt a connection to her since we both have southern backgrounds."

Lamon did not want to know the intimate details of what took place at the shoots. The couple needed money so he looked the other way. But the dual lifestyle began to take its toll on Amanda and once again the couple faced rock bottom.

Amanda told Lamon that she didn't want to do porn anymore. Lamon simply shrugged his shoulders and asked what can we do right now? His disability checks had not come in yet and they were pressed for cash.

Amanda would continue on in the porn business. She would accept a job in New York City for a company called Forbidden Gems.

It would be here that she would meet the man who would change her life forever.

Jason Andrews.

CON ARTIST AND GAY PORN STAR

Andrews worked as a disc jockey in Chicago and was known in the techno club scene as DJ Veritas. He was described as "obnoxious" and "brash", bragging about his military service in the United States Marines. He told everyone he was raised in Britain but was born in Israel.

Jason was popular among the velvet clubs of Chicago's Lakeview neighborhood, near Wrigley Field. He stated in his online bio that his music was based in the "grittiness of his UK elector roots." He talked with an exaggerated British accent and showed off a chiseled physique on his social media pages.

"He had girls and boys all around him," George Zelichowski said, a nightlife photographer. "They all just sort of fawned over him."

He also had a double life as a gay porn star.

Jason was reportedly straight but filed the homosexual scenes for the money, a term known as "gay for pay."

He also had a short fuse and would become "bitter or upset for no apparent reason."

He told Zelichowski that he had seen people killed ruing his time in the military but he would just stare off into the distance before going into detail.

"I have post-traumatic stress disorder," Andrews said. "Some of us know how to hide it pretty well."

During the film shoot for Forbidden Gems, Amanda because enamored with Andrews. She liked his accent and his charisma.

"The scene was that he was my boyfriend," Amanda said. "I never cared for any other partners. It was fake. This was fake. But my scenes with him were not. I liked his accent. He seemed so perfect."

The producers of the porn shoot took note that Amanda and Jason had become fast friends. They took their cigarette breaks together and slept in the same bed after filming had wrapped for the day. With the job now complete, both Andrews and Amanda decided to stay in New York for a little while longer.

RETURNING HOME

Lamon could sense the change in Amanda when she returned home. He wanted to repair the marriage. His disability checks were now coming in and he informed her that she no longer had to work in adult films.

He didn't realize, however, that Amanda found a new lover.

She would e-mail and text Andrews every day. She wanted out of the marriage.

Amanda went back home and took her daughter to her father's home in Florida. She then went to live with Jason Andrews much to her husband's dismay.

Lamon wanted to save his marriage but his wife would not hear it. She had once again descended down the path of darkness, this time she was accompanied by a man who gave her everything she wanted.

Drugs and sex.

With Andrews, Amanda only lived for the moment. The two used prescription drugs to fuel their marathon sex sessions at night. For money, Andrews continued working as a gay porn star. Amanda would work as a masseuse who would provide her clients with "happy endings."

The end goal for both was simply to get enough money to get high and have sex.

"There was passion," Amanda said. "We played around more. We talked more."

Lamon would come home to find Amanda packing her bags with a man he had never seen before.

Jason Andrews.

Lamon demanded to know what the hell was going on. Amanda brushed him off while Jason threatened to kill Lamon. He pulled a gun on his lover's husband and police were called.

"She's my wife!" Laman screamed at Andrews. "She's my wife, you piece of shit!"

Police would arrive and Laman would be humiliated in front of his former comrades. Cuckolded by a man with a British accent while his wife stuck up for her new lover.

Lamon was a nice man. He wanted to protect and provide for Amanda and her daughter. He thought these desires would be enough to entice Amanda to stay on the straight and narrow.

But with Jason, Amanda had drugs, sex, and danger.

"Jason would talk about other people's pain," Amanda said. "Going around and hurting someone. He wanted to do more than just play act. That is what got him off. Raping someone or killing someone."

"The perverse sex they engaged in was like a gateway drug," Orange said. "They needed something more and more extreme in order to get the same 'high' as they did before. Simulated rape would become real rape. Simulated killing would become real killing. They were on a slippery slope to oblivion and neither was very bright to begin with."

THE WAGES OF SIN

Dennis "Scooter" Abrahamsen wanted to have some fun.

He owned his own towing truck but had many other jobs on the side. He loved the strip clubs and worked as a bouncer there. Overweight with a sizable gut hanging over his belt, Scooter made his living primarily as a tattoo artist. When he had extra money, he would have female companions, strippers, come over to his home to entertain him. His neighbors reported seeing the young women coming and going out of his house whenever payday hit.

He was hanging out with another couple when he received a text from a woman he knew only as "Sunny Dae". She wanted to know if they could 'hang out'.

Never one to turn down a party, Scooter agreed. He went to the local 7-11 to get some cigarettes with the couple and returned home to prepare for the 'sex party' with the blonde porn star.

But Amanda had something other than a happy ending in mind for Scooter.

She texted Jason Andrews before she went to the party, detailing plans of how they would rob and kill Scooter.

Amanda arrived at the home and annoyed the other couple as she had her attention riveted to her Blackberry, texting Jason.

"They are fucked up doubt they going to-" Amanda texted.

"And him? Drunk or coked up?" Jason replied.

"Not sure yet drunk I know"

"Gotcha. Ill try and get comfy. May be here a bit!"

"Yep"

"Christ-I took another half so I can be patient! Dont worry theres anorher bar (Xanax tablet)"

'That's ok drink we can get more baby I' got some vynil gloves'

"I'm so glad you're really committed to this take. Keep eyes for a knife, etc for me! You badass. Sunrise comes quick round here."

Amber would reply back in a long, rambling text.

The talk and anticipation of killing Scooter made her "hot". She couldn't wait to kill the man and then have sex with Andrews after. The adrenaline rush got her excited.

The other couple would finally leave at 5 a.m in the morning. Amanda stayed behind and told Scooter to get on the massage table.

Jason Andrews rolled up in his car outside Scooter's home.

"Just get him on his face either bash or tell me to get in and. Where to go," Andrews texted.

"K I'm horny! I'm getting him to play music," Amber texted back.

"Wicked. I'll be waiting. Really. Take. Your. Time."

KILLING TIME

Jason would enter the home with a sledgehammer in hand and smash the unsuspecting Scooter over the head. He would hit him over a dozen times, splattering blood across the room.

Not satisfied that he was dead, Jason took a knife from the kitchen drawer and stabbed Scooter in the back over thirty times. He then took the murder weapons and dumped them in a laundry basket next to his victim.

The couple would then steal everything they could get their hands on. His laptop computer. Prescription drugs. Six thousand dollars in cash. Credit cards. A digital camera.

Fueled by drugs and adrenaline, Amanda and Jason drove to their hotel room where they had sex.

A day after the murder, Amber had messaged Jason's Twitter name 'Hearveritas' : "Taking it easy with hearveritas! Laying around eating popcorn and watching movies!"

Jason then went on the Twitter account himself and tweeted. "therealsunnydae and I wanna go watch a movie tonight, any suggestion?"

After the movie, they would go to a Home Depot in the next county over and use Scooter's credit card.

Scooter's body would not be discovered until that evening. His cousin Vincent Rella became worried that Scooter was not answering his texts. He went to Scooter's home and knocked on the door.

"I knew something was wrong," Rella said. "He would always answer the door for me."

Rella would enter the home and see his cousin laying face down, the room splattered with his blood.

It was a sight he would never forget.

The police initially thought that Scooter's murder could be a revenge killing. They knew that Scooter operated on the other side of the law sometimes. He hung out with strippers. Biker gangs. He repossessed cars.

This could be a case of someone killing him to get some payback.

Seeing the cop cars around the residence, the couple that had hung out with Scooter earlier decided to find out what was going on.

They informed the police of what took place at the home that night. They had been hanging out at a strip club called the Brass Flamingo with Scooter until he received a text from a woman named Sunny Dae.

All they knew was that she was a porn star.

They met at Scooter's home for the sex party, having intercourse in the hot tub. The couple noted that Sunny Dae looked bored and preoccupied throughout.

They left in the morning, leaving Scooter alone with the woman.

Investigators found Scooter's cell phone and traced his last calls. Interestingly, they did not find the number belonging to Amanda.

They found a number belonging to Jason Andrews.

Running a background check on Andrews, they discovered that he had been picked up for shoplifting earlier in the day with a blonde woman.

Her name was Amanda Logue, aka Sunny Dae.

Police interrogated both. They believed that Amanda was the killer and that Jason may have been a witness. Amanda remained guarded throughout the questioning. She was cool and calm, asking for a lawyer when the questions became too hot.

Jason chafed under the questioning. His hot temper flared when he was asked a simple question.

The couple posted bond and were released, however, as police didn't have enough evidence to keep them. They did have enough to get a search warrant for Amanda's white Ford Explorer. Inside, they found two different blackberry phones. The batteries and sim cards had been removed but they still hoped to be able to retrieve the messages by contacting Amanda's cell phone carrier.

With the heat now on, Amanda decided to part ways with Jason. She would return home to Leesburg, Georgia and beg forgiveness from Lamon.

Lamon would drive five hours to pick Amanda up. He had not heard from her in over three months but still loved her.

Once home, Amanda told Lamon bits and pieces of what happened. Lamon simply responded by hugging his wife.

"I told him after we got home," Amanda said. "He just held me."

She went to church that Sunday. She begged God for forgiveness.

But the investigators paid her a visit later that day, as detectives came to her home to question her about Scooter's murder.

Amanda would lie, telling him that Andrews killed him in a jealous rage after seeing her in the hot tub with him. She said that Andrews got all of the evidence, bloody knives, the hammer and surgical gloves and put them in a blue laundry basket.

Lamon thought his wife was only a murder witness. He immediately demanded to see a lawyer. But the detectives pressed the issue. It was in her best interest to tell the truth about what happened.

Amanda decided to try and save her own skin. She told police that Jason had "grabbed the back of her hair then twisted her arm behind her back." He then forced her to look at Scooter's crushed skull. He threatened her saying "that's what is going to happen to you if you tell anyone."

Amanda's story was convincing. She laid out all the narratives of an abused girlfriend. Jason had seduced her with this hedonistic lifestyle but then turned violent. Scared for her life, she didn't know what to do.

And Jason was distraught when Amanda left him. He would write on his Twitter account (in Hebrew language) : amanda please let me know if you are ok, really. My heart can't take the weight of the fear that I would never see you again."

But evidence technicians were able to recover the full extent of the text messages between Amanda and Jason. The messages were not deleted when she threw away the sim cards. They remained in the cell phone's memory chip.

The text messages were incriminating. Police immediately converged on Amanda's home.

She was more than a little surprised when they told her she was under arrest.

Amanda's demeanor of a tearful victim quickly changed. She cursed the arresting officer and began screaming at Lamon, telling him what to do.

It was further humiliation for the former cop.

Jason, meanwhile, remained at large.

It took two months but finally a tip from his current girlfriend led to his arrest. She googled his name and found out that he was wanted for murder.

He had left the Florida area and had found work in Chattanooga, Tennessee as a manager in a billiards club.

Police arrived at the club and found the British-accented Don Juan dressed like a cast member from Miami Vice.

He was shocked that they found him and told him he was under arrest.

A CON MAN FROM THE START

Jason was presented with all of the evidence and immediately cracked. He had been faking his British accent all along. He was an American citizen born and raised in Kansas. He reinvented himslef after his marriage ended in divorce.

Everything about Jason Andrews was fake.

Everything except the murder he committed.

"I was the one who swung the hammer," Andrews said. "More than a dozen times. I smashed his head in. I wasn't even shaking. I was a lot calmer than I am now. He was immediately knocked unconscious. I think that he didn't feel a thing after that. I pray that he didn't feel a thing. I really do."

Andrews asked for the death penalty.

"I deserve it," he said.

Pressed further, he had a different story to tell about Amanda. He wasn't abusing her. She was there for the fun of it.

"The motivation was robbery," Andrews said. "But if I have to be honest I think it was more about killing the man."

The excitement of murdering someone gave both Andrews and Amanda a sexual thrill.

Amanda had even texted Jason while she was having sex with Scooter in the hot tub, telling him how she couldn't wait for them to be together after the deed was done.

On July 21st, 2010, both Andrews and Amanda would be indicted on first-degree murder charges. The death penalty would be forthcoming.

Jason Andrews would reverse his initial request to be executed. Instead, he took a plea deal for life in prison. Amanda would get a 2nd-degree murder charge.

Her husband Lamon remains a faithful husband.

"I hope she'll get out," Lamon said. "She'll get out and we'll have some sort of family life."

Scooter's family, however, was not as forgiving or hopeful.

"You're not a person," Scooter's cousin, Donna Rella, said to Amanda during the trial. "He had a family. You have taken him away from us all."

"I hope anytime you close your eyes, he comes and haunts you for the rest of your pathetic life."

TAUSHA MORTON

AN AGGRESSIVE FLIRT

Dewayne Barrentine met Tausha Morton in early 2007.

She worked as a teacher's assistant at his son's daycare. A single parent, Barrentine would pick up his son and would be greeted by Tausha on a daily basis.

"Whenever I would pick him up," Barrentine said. "She would always make sure to step out into the hallway and give him a hug and say 'hey' to me. She made herself very noticeable."

Tausha gave Barrentine all of the hints that she was interested. The sideways glance, the smile that lingered just a little too long. But still, he needed extra coaxing.

"One of her co-workers actually approached me," Barrentine recalled when a woman in the hallway had passed him a note.

"She said, 'It's a phone number,' I said, 'To who?' She said 'Miss Tausha and she wants you go give her a call tonight. And it started from there."

Smitten by the forward nature of the sweet-faced single mother, Barrentine fell hard.

The two began dating and began living together within a month.

"She was really there for my son...," Barrentine recalled. "I had full custody of him. He would lay in the bed next to me ... and I would hear him say his prayers and he would pray for a mama." He would soon feel the same way about Tausha's daughter, Lexie.

"We weren't dating even a month and she said, 'Will you be my daddy?' And I said, 'Baby, I'll be whatever you want me to be...'"

From that moment, Barrentine became hooked as Tausha made him feel as if she really loved him. She did all the little things from kind words to love letters.

He soon began to realize, however, that Tausha had a manipulative, lying nature.

The tall tales began to pile up. She told Barrentine that she had a "Bachelor's degree in Criminal Justice" as well as an inheritance due to her from an inhertiance.

"It was from her granddad who was a federal judge who was blinded by a battery blowing up in his face. If he was a federal judge, surely his name would be on docs under Google somewhere, but I never found anything."

Barrentine grew increasingly suspicious with Tausha's stories. He did some online investigating and discovered that she had a previous marriage with a man named Mitch Kemp. He confronted her about it and she would state that she had been married five times before.

The two vaguely resembled each other, big Southern boys, "teddy bears" that were more than a little overweight.

After eight months of co-habitation, Barrentine caught Tausha cheating on him.

He promptly threw her out of his home.

"I called the Sheriff's department," Barrentine recalled. "I was like, 'look, I don't care what y'all do with her, she's got to get her shit and get outta my house.'"

Wanting retribution of some sort, Barrentine accessed Tausha's MySpace account as he knew her password.

"Dewayne gets on her Myspace account basically to mess with her," prosecutor Richard Hicks said.

After sifting through her e-mails, Barrentine would make a shocking discovery.

"I found two or three e-mails," Barrentine said. "And they were from Mitch Kemp's sister-in-law."

Mischele Kemp had written Tausha an e-mail with the subject "We're really concerned."

"How is Mitch doing? We haven't heard from you in over our year? We would like to hear from you. If we don't hear from you immediately we will contact law enforcement and media. It is not like Mitch to disappear for

years on end without contacting his mother and we have became extremely concerned. Please contact us. We are very worried about him and your entire family. Sincerely, MK."

Digging a little deeper, Barrentine looked into Tausha's "sent message" box and it did not appear that she had ever responded.

"Immediately, I changed the password on the account," Barrentine said. "To where she couldn't access it and I printed off all those e-mails."

His actions would prove to be something bigger than a missing persons case. He would bring all of this information to the local police chief in Florida who instructed him to keep things to himself as he sorted things out with the Boone County Sheriff's Department in Missouri.

WHO WAS TAUSHA MORTON?

Tausha Morton, AKA Tausha Fields, met Mitch Kemp in 2001 when she lived in Colombia, Missouri.

Mitch worked as a carpet installer and had been recently divorced after fourteen years of marriage.

"It wasn't long after he got divorced that he met Tausha," Mitch's brother Rick said. "I would say within months."

Despite their eleven year age difference, Kemp fell hard for the young and vivacious Tausha.

Tausha was the proverbial "people person." Most of her friends and neighbors described her as someone who would make you welcome and treat you as if you were a long lost friend.

"She was bubbly," said one of Tausha's former employers. "Friendly and inquisitive. She paid attention and asked lots of questions about you."

Tausha liked learning about other people. She, in turn, would be all too willing to share details of her own struggles.

"She told us how her whole family was killed in a car accident," Rick Kemp said.

Tausha had a way of getting people to feel sorry for her. She would come across as a heavily burdened individual who suffered a lot of tragedy. People listening to her story would feel compassion for her lot in life and do what they could to help her.

Mitch Kemp listened intently to Tausha's tales of woe, buying them hook, line and sinker. He wanted to help her. To be her rescuer, her knight in shining armor.

The two began to date and by September of 2002, Tausha gave birth to a baby girl.

Mitch loved kids and was ecstatic. He proposed marriage and Tausha accepted.

"They got married in Pensacola," Rick said. "It was a very easy wedding."

The marriage seemed to look okay from all observers. Mitch's family didn't have any misgivings about Tausha, her charm enabling her to get into their good graces, at least at first.

"She was a really sweet girl," Carole Kemp said, recalling her first meeting with Tausha.

But over time, his family began to notice a personality change in Mitch. Sister Mischelle stated that he wasn't "as playful as he used to be."

Family gatherings would "take a back seat to things that she wanted to do" according to Tracy Kemp, who blamed Tausha's ability to manipulate.

As work responsibilities increased for Mitch, things began to go south in their marriage very fast.

DOMESTIC LIFE AIN'T FOR ME

Bored that she was left alone with the baby, the high-strung Tausha needed an outlet.

She would arrive at her friend's gym, the Body Zone, with her baby in tow. Soon she began working part time at the fitness center.

It was there that she would meet Greg Morton.

Morton was more physically fit than Kemp but he fit the same profile psychologically. He had recently broken up with a longtime girlfriend and was be vulnerable to the manipulative charms of Tausha.

"Greg was despondent over his break-up," a family friend said. "But when he met Tausha, he kinda perked back up."

Tausha used the same seductive strategy on Morton as she used on Kemp. She detailed her tragic back story. She told him stories of being molested, of being raped.

She also told Morton in no uncertain terms that her marriage with Kemp was on the outs. Making herself look like the victim, she told Morton that Kemp had made her miserable. He was abusive, bothered her constantly and threatened physical harm.

"She told him a bunch of lies," one of Tausha's friends said. "She said she was getting him (Mitch) served, that they were getting divorced."

By February 2004, her allegations of physical abuse would be reported to the police department as Tausha filed assault charges against him.

"She said he abused her," Rick Kemp said. "By assaulting her, or slapping her or something."

Tausha informed police that she and Mitch had gotten into an argument. Then he hauled off and hit her.

Mitch Kemp would plead guilty to the charges and spend over a month in jail. Upon his release, he would be in for another surprise.

Tausha had moved out of the family home and moved in with Greg Morton, taking Lexie with her. Morton had own a farm outside of Colombia, Missouri, a sizable estate that he inherited from his step-father.

A custody battle then ensued between Tausha and Mitch for their daughter. The fight would get uglier by the day with daily phone calls between the two and their attorneys. She would refuse to allow Mitch to see Lexie and used the courts to prevent visitation.

But Mitch Kemp would not give up without a fight.

"If he had to go through the court system to do it, he would do it," Mitch's brother Rick said. "But that he was going to see his daughter."

Tausha would state that their divorce was finalized in August as the custody battle lingered on. She would then marry Greg Morton the same month.

But Morton had no idea what he was getting into and a "triangle" domestic dispute ensued.

Tausha had arranged to meet with Mitch in order to get some personal belongings. She drove in with Greg to the house of Mitch's friend where he was staying. Mitch confronted Tausha on the front porch where he immediately berated her, screaming insults.

Greg was waiting in the car at the time and went to intervene on Tausha's behalf. Mitch became further enraged and hit Greg over the head with a patio chair.

Retreating, Greg and Tausha sprinted back to the car.

Mitch, however, would disappear after that confrontation.

THE DISAPPEARANCE OF MITCH KEMP

It took awhile for Mitch's disappearance to hit home for his family members and friends. He was the type of man whom you would not hear from from awhile but would suddenly show up on the front porch.

He was dutiful about calling his mother Carole and when she didn't hear from him, she began to worry.

"We called the Boone County Sheriff's office," Rick Kemp said. "About two weeks afterward, probably. We told them that Mitch had disappeared."

The Sheriff's department did not think any foul play was involved. They offered assurance to the family that Mitch "probably didn't want to be found."

Boone County detectives came to that conclusion after they found out that Mitch was wanted for stealing some goods from a friend. They believed he disappeared in order to escape from repercussions of his actions.

Meanwhile, Greg and Tausha were living large. In late 2004, Greg put up his farm for sale which surprised both his friends and family. He treasured the land as it was bequeathed to him from his stepfather. Those close to him believed that Tausha had put him up to it.

In February of 2005, the sale of the farm finalized. With a $275,000 payout in hand, he and Tausha left Missouri, telling no one.

The Kemp family continued to believe that Mitch was not missing and that Tausha was involved somehow. They just didn't have any evidence or clues. Just a damn strong suspicion.

"Something had either happened to Mitch that had nothing to do with Tausha," Rick Kemp said. "Or something happened to Mitch and Tausha had something to do with it."

Both the Kemp family and Boone County law enforcement would then find locating Tausha and Greg to be a fruitless exercise. They literally disappeared from the face of the earth, wanting a new life. Leaving no trail behind, Tausha and Greg would move all the way to the Gulf Coast.

Greg, still smitten by Tausha, would get a tattoo of her name on his back as if he were a branded cow. With a new man firmly under her control, Tausha would go on a spending spree which included getting breast implants with Greg's money.

NO SIGN OF MITCH

By February of 2008, the Kemp family still had not heard from Mitch.

"They took a missing persons report," Rick Kemp said. "But the case went cold, quite frankly, because they didn't do anything about it."

But the Kemp family would not give up hope. They continued their search, turning to the Internet to look for any trace of their beloved son and brother.

They would search different social networking sites and court systems to look for any trace of Mitch.

They found nothing for years.

Until Mischelle Kemp found Tausha on MySpace, the social networking account.

"My sister-in-law found an account," Rick Kemp said. "That had Tausha's name and picture on it."

Mischelle immediately sent Tausha an e-mail.

"Tausha didn't respond," Rick Kemp said. "But Dewayne Berrentine did."

REVENGE SEEKING BOYFRIEND TO THE RESCUE

Dewayne Berrentine read through Tausha's e-mails on MySpace and began connecting the dots.

"Her little stories," Berrentine said. "Just because somebody lies to me, that doesn't mean I'm going to call you out on it immediately. I thought that she was coming up with these stories to impress me, maybe?"

Dewayne had discovered that Tausha had gotten around. He received some disturbing information from a man that Tausha had dated after she met Greg and before she met Dewayne.

His name was Keith Jones.

"I was in love with her and anything else didn't matter," Jones recalled. "You couldn't verify anything that she said," he says. "You know, and I mean there were a lot of stories."

Keith and Dewayne exchanged notes and stories about Tausha. They realized that she told them the same outlandish stories. But then Jones told Dewayne a story that he didn't hear before.

He described how Tausha revealed to him that she was involved in the murder of one of her exes.

"She had a few drinks in her," Jones recalled. "She said this guy had raped her and her daughter. And she apparently ... went to where he was and lured him back to her house ... and he walked in the front door. And that's when Greg shot him in the chest."

Both men thought the story was "so far-fetched" and because of the lies they always heard from her, thought nothing of it.

Dewayne did eventually confront Tausha about the allegation and she dismissed it out of hand, saying that her ex-boyfriend would say anything to throw a wrench into her new relationship.

Dewayne would change his mind about things when he opened Mischelle Kemp's e-mail message to Tausha, however. After notifying the authorities, he also wrote Mischelle Kemp back who in turn contacted the authorities in Boone County. The Sheriff's department then reopened the case. After doing some sniffing around, they discovered that Mitch had "fallen off the face of the earth" and had not filed taxes in over four years.

Finally, the Boone County Sheriff department realized that something was wrong.

INVESTIGATING TAUSHA

Detectives decided to start researching the background of Tausha.

They would discover that Tausha's parents were alive contrary to her account that they were both dead. Mitch's mother had spoken to Tausha's father shortly before her soon was to be married.

"She said, 'Mitch, we need to talk,'" recalled Rick Kemp. "You've heard a bunch of stories. Her family wasn't killed in a car wreck. They're alive. They don't want anything to do with Tausha. They say she's nothing but trouble."

Mitch dismissed the notion of his mother. He was totally smitten with Tausha.

Further investigations would reveal that Tausha had been married and divorced twice by the time she met Mitch Kemp. She would go onto have four marriages before she was thirty and the number of men she lived were numerous. Mitch had no idea that Tausha went from one man to the next man to the next. Even if he did, he was so smitten by her early in their relationship that he would have probably ignored the red flags.

Investigators would further discover that her divorce to Kemp was never finalized so she may have married Greg Morton while she was still married to Kemp.

Tracking her movements after she moved from Missouri proved difficult. Tausha and Greg were eventually tracked to Alabama.

The couple lived an indulgent lifestyle, buying luxury homes and cars on the $275,000 sale they profited after selling the farm.

But it didn't take long for them to blow through the money.

Needing more income to support Tausha, Greg would go to Mississippi in the hopes of finding clean-up work after Hurricane Katrina hit. After he left, Tausha saw it as an opportunity to cut him loose.

She had to find someone new.

"While he was gone doing Katrina," Barrentine said. "She was blowing through his money. Then he came home finding another man laying in his bed and he's broke."

Greg would immediately file for divorce.

MEN AND MORE MEN

Cut off from her money supply from Greg, Tausha would find work as an assistant at a day care center. It was there that she would meet Dewayne Barrentine.

She would follow the same modus operandi in her seduction of Barrentine, telling him the sob stories of her life. She described how Greg Morton would abuse her and how she escaped. She gave details on how Greg would try to "jump on her" and that they had "several physical altercations."

Agreeing to let her move in, Dewayne would meet Greg when he was helping Tausha get her belongings out of his house.

The two didn't fight. Instead, they spoke briefly and Greg would later tell Dewayne about how detectives from Missouri were looking to speak with Tausha.

Barrentine would eventually discover Tausha cheating on him and throw her out of his home. She would find a new boyfriend a few days later by the name of Denver Workman.

Workman left his job and his extended family from Florida to Wilmington, Delaware after Tausha begged him to do so. Then she wanted him to move back and Workman refused.

"She would yell, scream and throw things at me because I wasn't leaving," Workman recalled. "She would tell Lexie I was a bad person and to kick me. I bought her a bus ticket to Florida and let her borrow my truck that was still down there. She took the truck, and I never saw her again."

Police would finally catch up to Tausha in Dothan, Alabama and confront her about the disappearance of Mitch Kemp.

During her initial interrogation, Tausha would firmly deny having any contact with Mitch.

"What do you mean what happened to Mitch?" Tausha would ask detectives in bewilderment. "I haven't had any contact with him. None."

The investigators continued to press, however, and Tausha would try to insinuate Greg as having something to do with Mitch's disappearance.

"They had words on the phone," Tausha told detectives. "And then they had, they got in a fist fight one time."

After being threatened with the possibility of being put in jail and leaving her five year old daughter Lexie in the hands of the state, Tausha then placed the blame on Greg.

"Greg killed Mitch," Tausha said. "He told me."

She would then inform detectives that she wasn't there when it happened. She stated that Greg left about 45 minutes later after he had yet another phone conversation with Mitch.

Tausha would claim that she feared for both her and her child's life because of Greg's temper.

She would recall that Greg shot Mitch on the farm. Investigators played along, even paying for her plane ticket to fly from Alabama to Missouri in order to let them know where Greg had buried Mitch. But once she arrived, Tausha seemed confused by the layout of the farm. She could not pinpoint where exactly the body had been buried.

She was then released under her own recognizance back to Alabama while Sheriff deputies proceeded to dig up the farm to no avail. They used ground penetrating radar, cadaver sniffing dogs but came up empty.

WHERE WAS GREG MORTON?

While talks with Tausha revealed some clues, investigators were even more eager to speak with Greg Morton.

After ending his marriage with Tausha, he settled in St. Louis. He was going to school to become an electrician and had a new girlfriend.

He wanted nothing further to do with Tausha. When investigators approached him, Greg immediately invoked his right to an attorney and refused to speak further.

Detectives did not have enough evidence to charge him. But they had Tausha on the run and spoke to her again. This go around, they decided to employ a little psychological manipulation.

"But I tell you what," Detective Dave Wilson said while sitting across from Tausha in the interrogation room. "He (Greg Morton) automatically assumed that you talked to us. Now, we didn't confirm that."

"Why did he think that?" Tausha asked.

"Well, there's only...who knows?"

"But he said he thought he'd talk to you?"

"I'm going to ask you again. Can you take us directly to where that hole was?"

This go around, Tausha said yes. The Boone County Sheriff's department flew her in from Alabama yet again to Greg Morton's farm.

This time, Tausha led investigators straight to where the body was buried.

Mitch Kemp's remains were dug up and his identity was confirmed.

"It didn't surprise us," Rick Kemp said. "But we were all just blown away. I mean, I just didn't want to believe that my brother was gone."

Investigators discovered that Mitch had been shot numerous times and found numerous shell casings in the makeshift grave. They then went to St. Louis and arrested Greg Morton.

"He wasn't surprised when we showed up," Detective Wilson recalled.

Tausha was allowed to return home but investigators had a suspicion that she was more involved than she let on.

A VOW OF SILENCE

Greg strangely refused to rat out Tausha, remaining in prison until he was officially charged.

Tausha moved to Texas, however, and began dating someone new. Investigators would catch up with her again, however, and this time a heated ninety-minute interrogation would ensue.

Their probing questions would force Tausha to change her story about Mitch's murder completely.

"I did not do anything," Tausha said after detectives informed her that she would be charged with first-degree murder. "I helped you in every way I could possibly fucking help you.

"Tausha," Detective Wilson said slowly. "We got people who say, say otherwise, okay."

Tausha then changed her story again, stating that she was present when Greg murdered Mitch.

"I snuck around behind Greg's back and I saw Mitch, okay," Tausha said. "Greg had no idea."

She stated Greg would kill Mitch in a jealous rage after they returned from a hotel for a tryst. They then drove back to the farm and Greg assaulted Mitch before he got out of the car.

"He had a gun in his hands," Tausha said. "It was a black gun. Mitch started walking backwards. I ran inside the house and then I ran back outside. I saw that Mitch was walking backwards, and Greg was walking towards him. And Greg shot him. I didn't kill Mitch. I didn't want Mitch to die."

But the investigators didn't see it that way. They charged her with first-degree murder.

THE TRIAL

In June of 2009, Tausha had been imprisoned for over six months as she awaited trial.

Her bail was set at one million dollars.

Greg Morton then decided it was time to cut a deal. He broke his silence on what really happened the day of Mitch Kemp's murder. He would admit to his involvement in exchange for a more lenient sentence if he testified against Tausha.

In 2010, Tausha's trial began.

The prosecution's argument was that Tausha was the mastermind behind the murder, that even though Greg pulled the trigger it was Tausha that put the idea in his head. They also believed that Tausha's motive was to have sole custody of their daughter.

The defense would claim that Tausha was innocent and the victim. Her attorney was, in essence, using the same technique that Tausha used on all of her men. They would play on sympathy and hope that the jury would be as charmed by Tausha as all of her men.

GREG MORTON CONFESSES

Morton would take the stand and tell the jury exactly how Tausha manipulated him to kill Mitch.

"She's hysterical," Morton recalled. "She said Mitch raped her."

"What are you feeling, Greg, at this point?" Prosecutor Hicks asked.

"I wanted retribution. Tausha took charge and handed me a gun the net morning. She goes, 'I'm going to get Mitch, and when I get back, you shoot him.'"

"What were you going to do, Greg?"

"I was going to do what she asked me to do."

"They made a plan in that Tausha was going to go in town and pick Mitch up," Rick Kemp said. "And tell him that Greg was out of town."

Mitch arrived at the farm, thinking that it would only be the two of them. But then Greg emerged from the porch.

"I had a gun in my hand," Morton recalled. "I raised it and pointed it at him. I kinda paused I was kinda struggling with it a little bit. And then she started yelling at me to shoot him."

Greg believed that he was committing a protective act. He believed that Mitch was raping Tausha and molesting their six-year-old daughter.

"Then she said 'You got to get something to move him. Get something to move him with." Greg recalled. "Then she said, 'Come on. You should have had this ready.'"

"And you saw that she was still struggling?"

"He was."

"So what did you do?"

"I shot him again."

"Was he struggling anymore?"

"It was over," Morton said. "I used farm equipment to pick up Mitch's body and we buried him in a pit. When we were rolling the dirty on Mitch she said 'Mitch Kemp is a piece of shit and nobody is going to look for him for a long time.'"

The defense would then call a neighbor who testified on Tausha's behalf, stating that she thought she was under Greg's control.

Greg then broke down on the stand and tearfully apologized to Mitch Kemp's family.

Over time, however, he began to realize that Tausha was a cunning liar. As he got to know her better, he realized that he had been duped.

"He'd been played like a fiddle by her," Rick Kemp said. "She did it to every man that she had."

Tausha was not called to the stand by the defense and the jury would find her guilty.

"I think she thought she was going to walk," Rick Kemp said. "She thought she could just get away with lying and manipulating people."

Tausha Morton was sentenced to life in prison without parole but is currently appealing her sentencing.

CHRISTA PIKE

55

Christa Gail Pike, born 10 March 1976, currently sits on Tennessee's death row for the murder of Colleen Slemmer, 19, on 12 January 1995. The murder occurred when Pike was 18 years old. Pike and her then-boyfriend Tadaryl Shipp who was 17 at the time of the murder were convicted of Slemmer's murder and conspiracy to commit murder. Another friend of the defendants and the victim, Shadolla Peterson, also 18 at the time, was convicted as an accessory after the fact and given six years' probation after turning informant. Pike was sentenced to death by electrocution in 1996 and, at the time, she had the distinction of being the youngest woman ever to be sentenced to death, in any state and only the second women given the death penalty in Tennessee.

Early Life

Pike's life reads like a primer for depraved murderers. As a small child, Pike did not enjoy a healthy and supportive bond with her mother, Carissa Hansen, a licensed nurse, allegedly because of her premature birth. Whereas thousands of children are born prematurely and do not resort to criminal behavior Pike's birth was presented as evidence of one possible origin of her poor and troubled behavior. Pike's maternal grandmother was verbally abusive and Pike was raised by her alcoholic and abusive paternal grandmother until the latter's death in 1988 when Pike was 12; after which Pike attempted suicide by overdosing. She was then shuttled back and forth between her divorced parents' homes. In 1989, Pike was kicked out of her father's house for the second and final time due to her unruliness and the alleged sexual abuse of her father's then-two-year old daughter with his second wife.

Prior to the murder, experts assert that there were myriad indications that Pike was seriously disturbed; however, nobody who may have suspected this sought help for the increasingly disobedient and incorrigible young lady. According to Pike's mother, she was problematic since the age of eight and the two of them had a contentious relationship due to Pike's fluctuating and troubling behavior. Her mother asserted that by age nine Pike was growing marijuana in pots at their home and had been permitted to have a live-in boyfriend at age 14. At one point—in an effort to improve their relationship—Hansen suggested that she and Pike smoke marijuana together. Hansen mistakenly believed that cultivating a friendship with her daughter would cultivate the necessary bond Pike had been lacking her entire life. At one point, one of her mother's boyfriends whipped Pike with a belt which prompted her to wield a butcher knife against him before he was subsequently arrested. Hansen also admitted that Pike had repeatedly lied to and stolen from her. In several interviews with Hansen throughout Pike's trial and seemingly endless appeals, she admitted repeatedly that she was a terrible mother and should have spent more time with her daughter.

Pike's aunt, Carrie Ross, provided insight into Pike's upbringing when she testified that she disallowed her own children from associating with Pike because she lived in a filthy house that had zero ground rules and that Pike was a pathological liar of whom she was somewhat afraid. She also admitted that there was a history of substance abuse in Pike's family. Ross also stated that on the few occasions that Pike actually visited her she behaved like a little girl and engaged in Barbie and dress-up play with her eleven-year-old cousin. Further, there were some allegations that Pike may have been sexually abused but these were neither confirmed nor denied.

Pike's father, Glenn Pike testified that he did, in fact, kick his daughter out of his house multiple times; the last time being in 1989 after the aforementioned allegations that Pike sexually abused her two-year old half-sister. He admitted that he had signed adoption papers for Pike prior to her 18th birthday and that during the times she resided with him she was manipulative, disobedient, and dishonest.

After dropping out of high school, Pike began Job Corps classes in computer programming. Job Corps is a government-based organization that provides occupational and vocational training to underprivileged and troubled teens. It was at the now-defunct Job Corps center in Knoxville where she met Shipp, Slemmer, and Peterson. While Job Corps seeks to promote prosocial behavior and foster a strong desire among its participants to learn a vocation and secure a more promising future than might have been previously the case, this program is also known to cultivate criminal activity, likely due to the association among its participants; many of whom already had problematic behavior.

Evidence of Premeditation

On 11 January 1995, the day before the actual homicide, Pike told friend and co-Job Corps student Kim Iloilo that she was planning to kill Slemmer because she "just felt mean that day." Iloilo discounted Pike's statement as nothing more than merely talk; however, the following evening at approximately 8:00 p.m. Iloilo witnessed Pike, Shipp,

Peterson, and Slemmer leaving the Job Corps center. When Iloilo saw Pike, Shipp, and Peterson returning at approximately 10:15 p.m. without Slemmer she, again, thought nothing of it. Even when Pike visited Iloilo's dorm room at 11:00 p.m. that night and confessed to killing Slemmer—as well as showing Iloilo what Pike identified as a piece of Slemmer's skull—Iloilo still failed to tell anyone. Later, at Pike's trial, Iloilo testified that while Pike was iterating the events of the murder she was oddly smiling, singing, and dancing around the room. The following morning Iloilo asked Pike what she was going to do with the piece of skull. Pike nonchalantly replied that she had it in her pocket and was, in fact, eating breakfast with it.

Pike also told another student, Stephanie Wilson, a similar account the following day and proudly described the brown spots on her shoes as blood. Not unlike Iloilo, Wilson failed to immediately report anything.

The Crime Scene

On 13 January, officers from the University of Tennessee and Knoxville Police Departments were dispatched to greenhouses on the University's agricultural campus in Tyson Park where a University grounds department employee reported finding, at approximately 8:05 a.m., what he assumed to be a dead animal. The gruesome discovery was a corpse that turned out to be Colleen Slemmer. She was naked from the waist up; her throat was cut; her head had been bludgeoned; and she had various cuts all over her arms, throat, and torso—including a pentagram that had been carved into her chest. Officer John Terry Johnson who testified at Pike's trial described Slemmer's body as so badly beaten that she was unrecognizable as a human being. He also stated that he thought he was looking at her face when, in reality, Slemmer was lying face-down in the dirt and debris where Pike, Shipp, and Peterson had left her.

There was additional evidence and testimony that the crime scene encompassed an area that measured 100 feet long by 60 feet wide; an astounding 6,000 square feet in area. Despite the area being muddy and wet there was ample evidence of a physical struggle with trampled bushes, a considerable amount of blood, body drag marks, and hand and knee prints. Thirty feet from Slemmer's body was a large pool of blood which suggested that Slemmer was attacked in one area and then dragged to where her body was later found. Slemmer's shirt and bra were also discovered at the crime scene, as well as a bloody rag that Pike admitted to tying over Slemmer's mouth at one point to keep her from screaming.

Disturbingly, University of Tennessee police officer Harold James Underwood, Jr., who was the officer assigned to secure the crime scene, testified at trial that Pike and a few other females came to the scene between four and five p.m. the day of the discovery and before Pike was even considered to be a suspect. Underwood stated that Pike had asked why the wooded area was marked off, who the victim was, and whether police had any leads as to who the suspect or suspects were. He particularly recalled Pike's odd behavior—moving around a lot while giggling amusedly—and that she wore a necklace in the shape of a pentagram. The following day, during briefing when informed that the victim had a pentagram carved into her chest, Underwood reported Pike's behavior and necklace to his supervisors.

Autopsy and Findings

During Slemmer's autopsy, the medical examiner, Dr. Sandra Elkins, had to identify the victim's body from dental records because her head was so bludgeoned that she was unrecognizable. After cleaning up Slemmer's body which was clad only in jeans, socks, and shoes, and covered with dirt and twigs, Dr. Elkins began cataloging Slemmer's wounds. Due to the sheer number of wounds on her back, arms, abdomen, and chest, and the fact that following department policy which stated that each individual wound be assigned a letter of the alphabet, when Dr. Elkins reached double letters she, instead, individually catalogued only the most serious wounds and that there were innumerable other superficial and defensive wounds. Among the most serious cuts was a six-inch gaping wound across Slemmer's throat that was deep enough to penetrate the fat and muscles in her neck as well as the aforementioned pentagram. Additional injuries included fresh bruising which Dr. Elkins asserted was consistent with crawling.

Cause of death was ultimately attributed to blunt force trauma to the head. Dr. Elkins surmised that Slemmer's head was hit with the asphalt at least four times—two to the left side, one over the right eye, and one to the nose—which collectively resulted in multiple and extensive skull fractures. One of these blows was to the left side of Slemmer's head—which, according to Dr. Elkins, occurred with the right side of the victim's head against a firm surface. This blow only fractured her skull but also imbedded a portion of Slemmer's skull into her head and contained black particles from the piece of asphalt determined to be the murder weapon.

Even more tragic was Dr. Elkins' findings that none of Slemmer's other wounds would have rendered her unconscious and evidence of active blood flow around the wounds and blood in her sinus cavity indicated that Slemmer was alive during the severe torture she suffered before being killed.

Arrest and Confession

The police quickly connected Pike to the homicide thanks to the piece of Slemmer's skull discovered in Pike's jacket pocket. Pike had left this jacket hanging on the back of a chair in Job Corps Orientation Specialist Robert A. Pollock's office on 13 January after meeting with him about a misplaced ID card. Pike's jacket remained in Pollock's office from 4:00 p.m. on 13 January until 7:30 a.m. on 17 January. After learning over the weekend that Pike was a suspect in Slemmer's murder investigation, Pollock immediately gave the jacket to William Hudson, the Job Corps' safety and security captain who turned it over to Knoxville Police Department Officer Arthur Bohanan. At trial, Bohanan would testify that he found a small piece of bone in one of the pockets and presented it to Dr. Murray Marks, a University of Tennessee forensic anthropologist who was reconstructing Slemmer's decapitated skull and the piece in Pike's jacket pocket fit perfectly into an area where a portion of her skull was missing at the time of the victim's discovery.

When confronted with this evidence and subsequently arrested, Pike waived her *Miranda* protections and confessed to the murder and permitted officers to search her dorm room where the blood-soaked jeans she wore the previous night were found. Additionally, Pike led officers to a trash can at a nearby Texaco station on Cumberland Avenue where she had disposed of Slemmer's ID and a pair of gloves Pike had been wearing at the time of the homicide.

Pike's transcribed confession was 46 pages long.

In it, Pike admitted that there was animosity between Slemmer and her because Pike was convinced that Slemmer was a rival for the affections of her boyfriend, Shipp, and that Slemmer was trying to get Pike kicked out of the Job Corps program so she could have Shipp for herself. Pike also claimed that she had awakened one night to find Slemmer standing above her with a box cutter; however, there is no evidence of this allegation. Instead, Slemmer had repeatedly called her mother, May Martinez, to tell her she was afraid of Pike who she had awakened to find in her room and that she wanted to come home; to which Slemmer's mother said that she couldn't because she had signed a contract. Pike stated that she had only planned to fight Slemmer to stop her from running her mouth. On that fateful night of 12 January, Pike, Slemmer, Shipp, and Peterson signed the Job Corps logbook as they were leaving for an outing Slemmer believed was to smoke marijuana en route to a video store so that Pike and she could try to work out their problems.

When the group entered a tunnel at the edge of Tyson Park, Slemmer likely felt that something was not quite right and proceeded to ask Pike where they were going and whether there was, in fact, any marijuana. These questions irritated Pike who began the brutal assault shortly thereafter after they had gone deeply enough into the woods so that nobody could hear them that led to Slemmer's murder.

Pike confessed to initially slamming Slemmer's head into her knee and then throwing her to the ground where Pike continually punched, kicked, and slammed Slemmer's head into the concrete, screaming, "the bi*ch won't die" and that she wanted "to see [Slemmer's] brains flow." According to witnesses Shipp and Peterson, as Slemmer continued to plead with Pike to stop, Pike got angrier and more brutal. Slemmer offered to return to her Florida home, leave her belongings at the Job Corps center, and not tell anyone what happened; however, Pike became more enraged and yelled at Slemmer to be quiet because "it was harder to hurt someone who was talking to you."

In addition to the savage beating, Slemmer had been cut innumerable times with a box cutter and a mini meat cleaver (that Pike had allegedly borrowed from another Job Corps student) to her torso, arms, face, and back including having had her throat slit six times prior to the fatal blow that resulted from having her head crushed by a piece of asphalt. There was also a pentagram carved into Slemmer's chest; however, Pike asserted that Shipp had done that. Pike also confessed to "just watching Slemmer bleed" when the victim got up and tried to run away. Pike admitted to cutting Slemmer's back: "the big long cut."

After the murder, Pike stated that she and Shipp washed their hands and shoes in a nearby mud puddle to conceal the blood, dumped the box cutter, and Pike returned the meat cleaver to the person from which she borrowed it. This person has never been identified.

The physical evidence and co-defendant testimony suggested that the assault and murder lasted from 30 minutes to an hour and consisted of Slemmer repeatedly trying to get up and run away but was prevented from doing so by the co-defendants who also, as Pike testified, contributed to the physical assault by throwing rocks at Slemmer's head and holding her down so she couldn't run away. Later, Pike would testify that she heard voices in her head overriding Slemmer's continual screaming, telling her that she needed to prevent Slemmer from filing charges against her for attempted murder. Pike also admitted that at one point she thought she had heard a noise and went to investigate it to ensure that they were alone, as well as alleging that during the assault she heard Slemmer breathing in blood and jerking but did not let this assuage her anger as Pike continued her savagery.

Even more troublesome, a police video recorded after Pike's confession shows Pike smiling and providing extensive details about the crime at the crime scene, oftentimes mimicking her actions that evening. Many have said that her demeanor on the recording was eerily similar to that of a little girl who was excited and happy that she had experienced the best day of her life and had no problem talking about the events that transpired, the heinousness of her actions, and how she felt about it all.

The facts of the homicide are not nor have they ever been in dispute, thanks to an abundance of evidence. Pike's confession, and witness testimony at the trial.

Pre-Trial Examination

Prior to her trial, Pike was given a battery of assessment tests and examined by numerous psychiatrists including clinical psychologist Dr. Eric Engum who found her to be extremely bright as evidenced by an I.Q. of 111—in the 77th percentile of the general population—which he believed to be remarkable given her difficult childhood and lack of formal schooling beyond the ninth grade. Dr. Engum also found that Pike had excellent reasoning, problem solving, language, and analytic skills, and was also quite adept at paying attention, sustaining concentration, and sequencing information. Dr. Engum concluded that Pike was legally sane and had no brain damage which has frequently been demonstrated to cause violent behavior in some individuals.

Of particular interest was that Pike was found to be marijuana- and inhalant-dependent and also diagnosed with borderline personality disorder. Whereas there are some similarities between borderline personality disorder and antisocial personality disorder such as impulsivity, irritability, aggression, and a self-image that fluctuates between self-aggrandizement and despair, there are several differences.

Individuals with borderline personality disorder differ from those with antisocial behavior in that the former—which primarily affects females—is characterized by a lack of remorse, self-destructiveness, black-and-white thinking, alcohol and/or drug use or abuse, unstable relationships characterized by fear of abandonment and extreme swings between love and hate, difficulty in achieving academic and vocational goals, and are more likely to have been sexually abused; while the latter—which affects disproportionately more males—is characterized by a lack of affect and remorse, emptiness, and an ultimate goal of self-preservation.

Pike demonstrated all of the aforementioned characteristics of borderline personality disorder which makes it easier—but not justifiably so—to comprehend how her intense jealousy of Slemmer and fear of losing Shipp made her commit her atrocious acts. In addition to her fear of abandonment, Pike also abused drugs, was likely sexually abused, had contentious relationships, and displayed zero remorse. Dr. Engum surmised that Pike did not act with premeditation or deliberation in Slemmer's murder but, instead, in a manner that was consistent with borderline personality disorder. More simply, Pike had lost control. However, on cross-examination Dr. Engum admitted that Pike's deliberate luring of Slemmer, that she carved a pentagram in the victim's chest, that she brought weapons with her, and that she bashed Slemmer's head into the concrete does, in fact, constitute deliberateness.

That Pike was overjoyed and singing in Iloilo's room describing the murder while dancing around with the portion of Slemmer's skull Pike had taken as a trophy further supported Dr. Engum's diagnosis of borderline personality disorder because she had eliminated who she perceived was in competition for her boyfriend, Shipp, and, therefore, could continue her relationship with him. When questioned about the piece of skull Pike had taken, Dr. Engum said that Pike had no identity and her actions of taking and displaying the skull was a way to get recognition, no matter how misleading and distorted said recognition might be. In fact, after her conviction and sentencing Pike wrote a letter to Shipp which was intercepted by jail personnel that stated that even though she tried to be "nice" to Slemmer by bashing in her head instead of letting her bleed to death she was still sentenced to "fry."

The Trial

There was an abundance of evidence presented at the trial. Physical evidence consisted of crime scene photographs, autopsy reports, bloody clothing, and the piece of Slemmer's skull Pike had taken as a trophy. With respect to this skull piece, Dr. Elkins presented Slemmer's decapitated skull that was reconstructed by Dr. Marks to explain the victim's injuries. The skull presented at trial was complete except for a portion that was missing on the left side of Slemmer's skull. Dr. Elkins demonstrated that the piece of skull found in Pike's jacket fit perfectly into this spot, much to the chagrin of Slemmer's mother who, in a taped interview, stated that Pike was oftentimes giggling and passing notes to her mother and defense attorney during the trial, not unlike an immature middle-schooler.

At the trial, the State introduced photographs taken of Pike and Shipp at the Knoxville Police Department in which both were wearing pentagram necklaces similar to the shape carved into Slemmer's chest. It was presented that both Pike and Shipp dabbled in devil worshiping and other forms of the occult and that Slemmer was a sacrifice for the next day, Friday the 13th. Despite the presence of some type of satanic elements in Slemmer's murder, Dr. William Bernet, Vanderbilt University's psychiatric hospital medical director, testified that the evidence was that of "an adolescent dabbling in Satanism." He further concluded that the concept of collective aggression—or mob mentality—in which a group of people become stimulated and subsequently engage in some type of violent behavior was most assuredly at play in the events leading to Slemmer's death. However, Dr. Bernet ultimately stated that he did not have enough evidence to definitively surmise whether Pike had acted with premeditation or intent when she lured and murdered Slemmer.

Pike was ultimately convicted of first-degree murder and conspiracy to commit first-degree murder after a mere two-and-a-half hours of jury deliberation. The fact that the jury returned guilty verdicts for first-degree murder—and did it so quickly—demonstrate that jurors were convinced that Pike had the requisite mens rea, or mental capacity, to warrant a first-degree murder charge: premeditation and deliberation. Amidst the overwhelming evidence and utter lack of remorse for her actions Pike was sentenced to death by electrocution (Tennessee has since adopted lethal injection for executions but has the prerogative to utilize electrocution if the lethal injection drugs cannot be obtained). Shipp was sentenced to life without parole because his age at the time of the murder was too young to warrant capital punishment and Peterson turned informant and was given six years' probation for her testimony.

Pike's conviction was upheld by the Court of Criminal Appeals and the United States Supreme Court denied certiorari.

Post-Conviction

While incarcerated, Pike demonstrated more evidence of her depravity. In 2001 she tried to murder fellow inmate Patricia Jones by strangling her with a shoelace. Pike alleges that Jones repeatedly tortured her by calling her "fried chicken" and making various demeaning sounds as an affront to what Jones said was the sound that Pike would make when she was electrocuted. The final straw was when Jones physically threatened Pike's friend, fellow devil worshiper Natasha Cornet. Pike said that she jumped atop Jones and choked her with a shoelace so that the much larger and heavier Jones would get off of Cornet. By the time prison guards reached them, Jones was unconscious.

Pike was subsequently convicted of attempted murder despite her prior death sentence because any offense committed while an individual is incarcerated must be adjudicated. During this time, neurology specialist Dr. Jonathan Henry Pincus began investigating Pike's brain to glean some type of knowledge as to why Pike behaved and continued to act violently the way she did when she assaulted Jones. He asserted that every killer he has ever examined share three commonalities: brain damage, a history of abuse, and mental illness. Dr. Pincus alleged that Pike did, in fact, possess all three features and demonstrates all of the requisite features common to serial killers. There is much consensus among professionals that Pike would likely have been a serial killer had she not been caught the first time.

He also testified at Pike's attempted murder trial that her brain's frontal lobes are not "put together properly"; largely due, he claimed, to the fact that Pike's mother drank while she was pregnant with Pike despite denial of this by Pike's mother. It was also brought up that as a child Pike played at the slaughterhouse where her grandfather worked and that she was frequently subjected to pornography and horror movies on the home television screen. He asserted that all of these factors provide insight into how an 18-year old girl could act with such depravity as was the case when Pike murdered Slemmer. However, the original trial judge, Mary Beth Leibowitz, stated that Pincus' "findings" of brain damage was curious as the defense expert at Pike's original trial who was trying to spare her the death penalty failed to find such evidence.

Forensic psychiatrist William Kenner testified that Pike had suffered from undiagnosed bipolar disorder, the symptoms of which were evident from the time Pike was a "sleepless, talkative adolescent" and likened her to an automobile with cruise control set at 120 miles per hour. Pike's post-conviction defense team alleged that this non-diagnosis justified her requesting a new trial.

In 2002 Pike sought to have her appeal legally stopped and to proceed with her execution. In June of that year Judge Leibowitz granted Pike's request and scheduled an execution date of 19 August 2002. However, a few days later Pike changed her mind and the Tennessee Court of Appeals subsequently stayed her execution. In October 2005,

Pike's death sentence was affirmed; however, no execution date has been set at this time.

Pike was again in court in 2007 when her defense team headed by Donald E. Dawson asserted sought a new trial, alleging ineffective assistance of counsel in that her trial defense team failed to introduce evidence supporting Pike's alleged bipolar disorder. During this hearing, Shipp admitted to misinforming investigators and that he, in fact, was primarily responsible for Slemmer's murder. He stated that he was drunk and tired and just wanted the police to leave him alone when he put the onus of blame on Pike. Additional testimony from prior Job Corps student and the defendants' mutual friend Tyrone Comfort stated that Shipp controlled and abused Pike despite her assertions that he was the first male to protect her and she admired the respect and fear he elicited from others. Pike, however, was heavily medicated during this hearing for her alleged bipolar condition and the hearing was rescheduled for April 2008.

During her 2008 hearing, prosecutors portrayed Pike as a cold-blooded vicious killer who not only planned Slemmer's murder but prolonged it for sport, essentially playing cat-and-mouse with Slemmer by allowing her to get up and try to escape and then pushing her back on the ground for additional torture. Ultimately, her request for a new trial was denied.

Pike became newsworthy again in 2012 when she formulated an escape plan with the help of 34-year-old New Jersey resident Donald Kohut who frequently visited Pike in prison but the extent of their relationship remains unknown, and 23-year-old former prison guard Justin Heflin. In a joint investigation by the Tennessee Department of Corrections, the Tennessee Bureau of Investigation, and the New Jersey State Police after receiving information about the plan, both men were arrested and charged with bribery and conspiracy to commit escape, with Heflin charged with an additional facilitation to commit escape charge due to his job as a prison guard. Authorities discovered contraband evidence in the facility which could have only been brought in by a staff member and that Heflin was likely involved. Further investigation demonstrated that Heflin knew Kohut and that Heflin was receiving gifts and money for his assistance in the escape plan. Pike was also charged.

Even more recently, during yet another post-conviction relief hearing in 2015, testimony revealed that Pike was allegedly pregnant at the time of the murder. While this may be true it neither excuses her actions nor provides any potential evidence of legal insanity to justify an affirmative defense of not guilty by reason of mental disease or defect or guilty but mentally ill. Also during this hearing, Slemmer's mother requested the missing piece of her daughter's skull so she could bury the whole of her daughter but was denied as the skull piece remains a critical piece of evidence in Pike's ongoing legal appeals.

Since exhausting the state appeal process, Pike's new defense attorney, Assistant Federal Defender Stephen A. Ferrell, filed a 123-page petition on her behalf alleging that he constitutional rights were violated in both the original 1996 trial and penalty phase and that Tennessee's appellate courts ignored said violations. Among these claims is that capital punishment would amount to cruel and unusual punishment in violation of the Eighth Amendment of the United States Constitution because of Pike's youth, immaturity and mental illness. While Shipp—only 17 at the time of the murder—was too young to warrant imposition of a death sentence, Pike was not. Ferrell alleged that her trial lawyers were incompetent and failed to introduce evidence of mental illness, brain injury, and post-traumatic stress disorder. In response, the state Attorney General submitted a 90-page rebuttal repeatedly asserting that the state courts' ruling were all legally correct. As of the beginning of 2016, this battle continues.

Numerous video interviews of Pike over the past several years show her admitting that she was fully cognizant of her actions and that they were wrong. She stated that she felt as though she was taking out years of abuse on Slemmer and that she committed a horrible atrocity and deserves to be punished; however, she asserts that she deserves life without the possibility of parole for her actions; not the death penalty for the actions of three individuals. She has repeatedly stated that she wishes it was she who died and not Slemmer but such protestations are moot after the fact. One cannot help but wonder if Pike actually means what she says or is simply saying what she thinks others want to her. Knoxville Police Department detective Randy York who worked the case has said that in his lengthy career he has not encountered many people who he believes are evil but that Pike is, indeed, the personification of evil and that she should never be permitted to be around other human beings ever again.

Experts assert that the death penalty is not an effective general deterrent and debate over the morality and legality of capital punishment remains contentious and in the forefront of public discourse and debate. Currently, Tennessee is only one of 38 states which have the death penalty. Whereas women comprise 13% of those arrested for murder, only 2% are sentenced to death and, of those, only 3% are actually executed; primarily due to judges not wanting to sentence women to death. In Tennessee, only two individuals on death row have been executed—both males. The last time a woman was executed in the state was in 1837. Many currently believe that Pike will likely never be executed.